DATE DUE

DE 6 '91	NO 19 99		
FE 7 '92	DE 1 8 99		
	DEC 0 00		
NO 30 '92	OC 6		
FE 19 '93	DE 1 1 00		
DE 1 7 '93	AP 6 '02		
JA	AP 25 '02		
AP 8 '94	AP 25 0		
DE 2 3 '94	6 '02		
NO 3 '95	MY 31 0		
DE 1 '95	NO 1 2 0		
MY 10 '96	DE 1 '03		
	MY 16 0		
MY 11 '	1 6 '0		
	FE 0		
DE 2 '00			
AG 5 '99			
AG 5 '9			

DEMCO 38-296

VGM

DROPPING OUT OR HANGING IN

DROPPING *OUT* OR HANGING IN

What you should know
before dropping out of school

Duane Brown

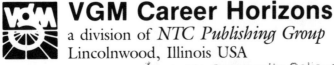

VGM Career Horizons
a division of *NTC Publishing Group*
Lincolnwood, Illinois USA

Library of Congress Cataloging-in-Publication Data

Brown, Duane.
    Dropping out or hanging in : what you should know before dropping
out of school / Duane Brown.

        p.   cm.
    ISBN 0-8442-8687-7 : $5.95
    1. High school dropouts—United States.   2. High school students-
-Counseling of—United States.   I. Title.
LC146.6.B76   1990
373.12'913'0973—dc20
                                                                90-32012
                                                                CIP

Published by VGM Career Horizons, a division of NTC Publishing Group.
© 1990 by NTC Publishing Group, 4255 West Touhy Avenue,
Lincolnwood (Chicago), Illinois 60646-1975 U.S.A.
All rights reserved. No part of this book may be reproduced, stored
in a retrieval system, or transmitted in any form or by any means,
electronic, mechanical, photocopying, recording or otherwise, without
the prior permission of NTC Publishing Group.
Manufactured in the United States of America.

0 1 2 3 4 5 6 7 8 9 VP 9 8 7 6 5 4 3 2 1

CONTENTS

FOREWORD

If you are thinking about dropping out of school, you should keep in mind that making such a decision requires a great deal of thought. It's simple to say, "I'm dropping out," but it may be very difficult learning to live with the consequences of such a decision.

There are certainly some people who have dropped out of school and gone on to lead very happy and successful lives. As this workbook points out, Ted Turner, millionaire owner of WTBS in Atlanta, and Peter Jennings of ABC News both dropped out of school and have done very well for themselves. However, for every success story, there are dozens of others that don't end as happily.

This workbook explains that, whether or not you decide to drop out of school, you have to learn to plan your immediate future as well as plan the long-term direction of your life. You will learn how to make decisions and how to take hold of your life by setting goals and achieving them.

We hope this workbook serves you well and that it helps you make an intelligent decision about dropping out of school or hanging in there until you finish.

The Editors
VGM Career Horizons

1

DROPPING OUT OF SCHOOL—THE DIFFICULT JOURNEY

You have probably taken many trips in your life. Sometimes even the shortest trip goes badly. You have an accident or a tire on your car goes flat. Or when you get to the place where you are going, you find that it really isn't the right place after all. You either can't buy the things that you want, the movie that you expected to see isn't showing, or something else is wrong. You've wasted a trip.

Life is also a trip. Not the type of trip that people who get high on drugs mean, but a journey. At any point in the trip of life, you are headed toward an uncertain place—a destination. You don't know what you will find at the end of your trip—or at any place along the way. You just hope it will be nice.

Going to school is one way to get ready for your trip to an unknown place. Going to school is like checking your oil or making sure you have enough gasoline to get where you want to go on an automobile trip. If you drop out of school, you will still make the trip of life. Dropping out of school may mean that you are not well prepared for your trip. It may mean that your trip will be harder than it needs to be.

Perhaps you are thinking of quitting school. Or your teachers, parents, and counselors are afraid you will quit. Many students do quit school. About one in four high school students drop out, although many of them later graduate from high school. But dropping out *now* is serious business.

This book has been put together to help you think through your decision to leave or stay in school. If you do decide to leave, people around you want to help you make plans so that later, if you decide to return to school, you will know what to do.

Most students drop out of school in their heads before they move their bodies out the door. These students are called *mental dropouts*. You can tell who they are. They don't care about school. They don't listen in class. They may sleep or fight while they are in school. They may not come to school very often.

Are you a mental dropout? Is your body in school and your mind somewhere else? If so, you need to read this book carefully. Not so you will stay in school. You may. But if you are "already gone," this book will help you prepare to come back to school if you decide to do so later. Yes, you may be back even if you drop out. About 40 percent of the students who drop out come back. That's 4 in 10. We will talk about why this happens later.

Mental dropouts can change their minds. So can students who are just thinking about leaving school. You can drop out, stop out, or stay in. Regardless of what you do, you need to be prepared.

WHY DO STUDENTS LEAVE SCHOOL?

There are almost as many reasons why students leave school as there are students. See if you can identify yours from the list below:

■ *School doesn't have anything to do with life. This stuff that I'm learning doesn't help me in life.*
Many lines from popular songs make fun of school, teachers, books, and studying. Lots of people, including some of those students who do well, think that history,

English, biology, and physical education won't really matter in their lives. They believe, sometimes correctly, that they can go out and make lots of money without finishing high school. Some West Virginia dropouts get jobs in the coal mines making over $15 per hour. Some don't.

■ *I'm always failing.*

For some, school is one failure after another. They get kicked and then stepped on by teachers and parents. The feeling you get is that you are no good because you are not doing well in school. It's hard to keep up the fight when the result is getting yelled at. Or maybe something worse happens. Maybe nobody notices you, even when you fail.

■ *My friends are dropping out.*

Some students decide to leave school because their friends are either leaving or have already quit. Some of you have heard your mom or dad ask, "If your friends jumped off a cliff, would you jump too?" Well, some of you would. School can be a lonely place without your friends.

■ *I'm pregnant.*

A lot of young women find themselves in the position of being pregnant and trying to finish school. This is a *tough* situation. Preparing to have a baby is difficult enough without having to worry about homework and class participation.

■ *I need money.*

Lots of students leave school because they need money for a car, clothes, rent, food, and for other reasons. They take jobs to pay the bills. Often these jobs become more important than school. Some students just cannot do both—work and be a student.

■ *School is boring.*

Some teachers aren't very interested in students and don't do a good job of teaching. Books are boring. Homework assignments just don't make any sense. The hours drag. The days seem to last forever. All you can think about is getting out. School is boring for a lot of people a lot of the time. Some put up with it. Others don't.

■ *I can't do the work.*

Some high school students have not learned to read or do math well. They are unable to do the most basic schoolwork. Not only do they fail, but they think that they will never be able to pass. They see themselves as dumb and unable to learn. Instead of asking for help, they quit.

■ *I'm too lazy.*

Some students quit school because they are too lazy to do the work. For some, they just don't see any reason to do the work. For others, they see the reasons, but they just won't do what needs to be done.

■ *I'm getting married and I will be a housewife. I don't need an education for that.*

A few students, mostly women, decide to get married and chuck school. They sometimes see marriage as a way to escape from school or home and expect to live happily ever after. Sometimes they do.

■ *My teachers are prejudiced and so is the whole school.*

Some students feel that they are treated badly because of their race or religion. Some schools have mostly black students in the less challenging courses. Some teachers do not like Hispanic students. In many instances, these students are right. School can be a place where not everyone is treated the same.

■ *Nobody cares.*

A lot of students who leave school complain that nobody cares about them. They go through entire days when no one speaks to or even notices them. Sometimes they do crazy things to get noticed. And that may work. But sometimes it doesn't. "It's hard to keep on trying when nobody gives a damn," said one student. He's right.

■ *Drugs or alcohol make it impossible to study.*
Life can be an endless trail of highs and lows, drunks and hangovers. Nothing matters for these students. Certainly not school!

THE OTHER SIDE

You've heard all the lectures about staying in school. *Everybody* says it's a good idea. Well, this isn't going to be a lecture— just some facts. We know that adults often collect information that supports decisions that they have already made. If you have decided to drop out of school, you will probably not pay much attention to what is going to be said here. However, try to stick with us anyway. There may be some facts that will shake you up a bit.

"School doesn't have anything to do with life." You are mostly right—what is taught in your classroom doesn't have anything to do with the way you live. But some of what you learn in school has a lot to do with life. In today's world, if you cannot read, at least at the sixth-grade level and do basic math, you are going to be lost on most jobs. You won't even get most jobs. Information about jobs of the future shows that workers are going to have to be *more educated*. They are going to need basic skills in reading, writing, and mathematics.

You also need to know that people who hire new workers think school is important. They think that if you cannot do the work in school, you cannot do their job.

Finally, the military will not take you unless you graduate and can demonstrate that you have good academic skills. You have to pass a test called the *Armed Services Vocational Aptitude Test* before you can get into the military.

"I'm always failing." Failing is frustrating. Maybe it's a reason for quitting. Why not? Just give up on yourself and school! Did you know that young people (18–23) who had poor academic skills were 5 times as likely to be at the poverty level as those who had good skills? Poverty is an ugly word,

but it is an uglier situation. Being poor means paying what money you have for rent and food and never having money for the things you would like to do. It means not giving your children what they need. It can mean unhappiness in many, many ways.

"My friends are dropping out." So you want to be with your friends. Would you ask your friends to do something that would cost them $4,000–$7,000 a year for the rest of their lives? Yet, some students urge their friends to drop out of school. Why? Because they are doing it. The old saying, "With friends like that, who needs enemies?" comes to mind here.

We have observed that many teenagers are pressured by their friends to drop out. We have also observed that black males receive the most pressure. The reasons for this aren't clear. If you are a black male, you should be asking yourself why your friends want you to leave school when it is unlikely that you will be able to get a full-time job—or even a part-time job. Across the country, only 40 percent of the black dropouts under age 20 were employed, according to a survey. Only $1/8$ of these were working full time. The picture doesn't get much better when you get older.

"I'm pregnant." If anything, pregnancy is a good reason to stay *in* school, not leave it. With a child, you are going to need *money.* If you work full time (which is unlikely) at a minimum wage job, you are still going to be poor. You and your child are going to have to do without. Of course, there are forms of help for you and your child. But the facts are that this help will not provide the kind of future you want for your child.

"I want money." A lot of teenagers own cars, want great clothes, need money for dates, and even provide support for their families. Let's face it, you may be able to make money working at a low-paying job. A full-time job will bring in about $175 a week before taxes are taken out. That means that you would earn about $7,000–$9,000 per year. However, of all dropouts under 20, only 55 percent are able to work full-time. Look at how much men earned in a recent year:

Dropouts	$ 6,725
High School Graduates	10,720
Some College	10,756
College Graduates	13,502

Figures for females were not available, but they would probably be about the same. Women, however, often earn less than men.

You need money now! If you drop out and stay out of school, you are probably going to be needing money *for a very long time.*

"School is boring." You are so right. A lot of things that go on in school are very uninteresting. But consider the alternatives. Is your current job, if you have one, fun? What if you had to stay on that job 40 to 50 hours per week? Would that turn you on? Probably not—but right now, it may look better than school. Here's a question for you: What are you doing to make school interesting? More about this later.

"I can't do the work." Very few people who attend school do not possess the ability to do schoolwork. Some cannot! They started getting behind in elementary school and just never caught up. Others never developed study habits. Still others have learning problems in understanding directions, or their brain reverses the things that they see. Poor basic skills can be corrected. This takes work. Study skills can be learned. Learning problems can be corrected or you can learn to cope with them.

But think of what happens when you don't learn. Students who do not are:

- 8.8 times more likely to leave school without a diploma.
- 8.6 times more likely to have a child out of wedlock.
- 5.4 times more likely to be on welfare.
- 5.0 times more likely to be at the poverty level.
- 3.6 times more likely not to be involved in anything meaningful.
- 2.2 times more likely to be arrested.

There is not a direct relationship between these kinds of problems and not learning. These figures only mean that those people who have poor reading, writing, and math skills are more likely to have other problems.

"I'm too lazy." School is work. Just getting out of bed, getting ready, and sitting through six hours of classes takes energy. How nice it would be if you could just get a few more "winks." But what happens if you drop out? Will you be able to sleep in? Will your parents support you? Probably not. You are going to have to (forgive the four-letter word) *work.*

Not long ago, there was a commercial on television that showed an auto mechanic explaining that you need to care for your car or it will break down. He ended the commercial by saying, "Pay me now or pay me later." We could say about school, "Work a little now and work less later." It is a basic truth that the worst jobs require the hardest work, are the most likely to end, and pay the least. If you truly are lazy, just remember that a little work now will save you a lot of work later.

"I'm getting married and I will be a housewife." The fact is that few women stay at home and keep house anymore. Only one in ten of all homes have a mother who stays at home, a father who goes off to work, and children. In fact, most wives work because the family needs the money. They continue to work when their children are born. Nearly 70 percent of mothers work, at least part-time.

Then there is the divorce rate. About one-half of all marriages end in divorce. Most of the time, the women are left with the children. There are about 12 million families below the poverty level headed by women. Young women must think of education as poverty insurance. Good jobs require a good education.

"Schools discriminate." There is often some truth to this charge. Discrimination, of course, is unfair. But it is a part of our society, one that we are working on. Prejudice will be around for a long time. The question is, should a person who is being hurt by it give in and drop out?

There is always the chance that your views are wrong. There may not be discrimination in your school. Teachers like students who try, who do their homework, who act interested. Maybe teachers treat you the way they do, not because you are black or Hispanic, but because you come to their class and don't do anything.

"Nobody cares." It is certainly true that a lot of teachers, counselors, and administrators appear not to care about many of the students. They are always too busy for you. Only the good students seem to get any attention. That's a problem in today's schools.

But have you asked anyone for help? Have you *insisted* that you be helped? You have the same rights as every other student. It is your right to be noticed—helped. And the counselors will help you if you ask. A lot of students think counselors just do work with students going to college. That is not so. If you feel like you are sinking, go to your counselor.

"Drugs and alcohol are more important than school." Drugs are used by some students to escape from school, home, from the bad things in their lives. They are used by others to get attention. Still others use them to make sure they are accepted by their friends.

Drug and alcohol abusers cannot be helped until they take the first step: admitting they have a problem. You have a problem if drugs and alcohol are more important than friends, family, and self-respect. If you don't like school, it's easy to deal with it by abusing drugs. You have to decide if you want to change that.

DROPPING OUT OR HANGING IN?

That's the end of the facts. You may have learned a few things about dropping out of school. Chances are that you are not convinced to stay in school by the facts presented. Potential dropouts are like potential traffic victims. They do not believe that anything bad will happen to them. They may be right. You may be right to think that dropping out of school will not end in a disaster. It didn't for Ted Turner, millionaire owner of WTBS in Atlanta. It didn't for Peter Jennings, who earns well over a million dollars a year as news reporter for ABC. And there are countless numbers of sports and entertainment figures who never completed high school and are doing well—better than well, actually. You may have the looks of Bo Derek (she dropped out), the athletic skill of Michael Jordan (he graduated from college), or the musical talent of Dolly Parton, who gives a cash award to every student who graduates from high school in her home county in Tennessee. You may be rich. Your parents may have decided to support you for the rest of your life. You may also be lucky.

Certainly, luck plays a role in our lives. Some people are in the right place at the right time. America is the land of opportunity. You just may run into one of those golden chances. You may win the lottery in your state and be set for life. Or you may not!

For the moment, set aside your current thinking about school. Set out, instead, on a journey in which you look at yourself, at school, and at your future both in school and out of school. You may decide after the journey that quitting school is the right thing to do. That's fine. You may also decide that staying in school is the better choice. That's fine too. But, regardless of what you decide, you need a plan to succeed.

Making a decision is only half the battle. Having a plan to make your choice work for you is the other half. We are convinced that many students would quit school if they knew what to do. We are also convinced that many more students would stay in school if they knew how to deal with school. The trip that you are about to take is for both groups.

This book is written with a bias. If it isn't clear already, here it is. Most students should stay in school *and* develop a good set of academic skills. This doesn't mean making straight A's or taking a lot of college prep courses. It does mean grabbing the opportunities offered by your school. This book can help you see some of the things you need to learn. It will also show you how to make school work for you instead of against you. But you will have to do some work. (There's that four-letter word again.)

Many of you will drop out of school for the reasons you have already identified. Many of you will want to drop back in as the problems of the life of a dropout become clear. If, at some point, you do drop out, have a plan to reenter school. Your choice to drop out may turn out to be the wrong one.

WHERE WE ARE GOING

What lies ahead are several exercises that will require you (1) to look at yourself as a student and as a person, (2) to learn some basic decision-making skills, (3) to make a choice about staying in school, and (4) to develop some ways of acting on this decision and some other choices if it turns out to be the wrong decision. These four steps will take a little time and some work. We have tried to make them as interesting as possible (for those who get bored), as easy as possible (for those who are lazy), and as meaningful as possible (for those who do not want to waste time). Finishing these exercises won't make you better looking or smarter or anything except *better* prepared to deal with school and life.

2

WHAT KIND OF PERSON AM I?

Every person is different. Every person looks different. Every person feels different. Every person thinks different. In this chapter, we want you to explore what you think and believe. We also want you to find sources of faulty thinking. That's right, people make mistakes in the way they think all the time. You've seen them do it! You know that teachers, parents, and others make mistakes in what they think about you, young people, cars, and the world. Well, if they do, what makes you sure you are always right in the way that you think about things? Jump in!—Let's look at some of the things you may or may not believe.

ARE YOU IN CHARGE OF YOUR LIFE?

How many times have you said, "It's my life. I want to live it my own way."? Most of us say that from time to time. Think back to the times when you wanted to do your own thing. At the same time, you've probably also said things like: "I wish my mom and dad would not be so bossy." Or "Teachers mess up my life. What do they know?" When we say such things, usually we are feeling angry. We think others are running our lives for us. They are always making us do things, whether we want to or not.

Let's get one thing clear at the start. You are living your own life! You are responsible for the good and bad things that happen to you. Unless someone picked you up and carried you to school today, you came on your own. But, you are probably saying, if I had not come, bad things would have happened. And, of course, you are right. There would have been *consequences. Consequences*—remember that word. We are going to be talking a lot about consequences. There are good and bad consequences that come from our choices. Sometimes we act to escape bad consequences. Sometimes we do things that will bring positive results. But, more importantly, *we do choose.*

Did you come to school this morning to escape your parents' anger? Or to escape the boredom of staying home? If so, you acted to avoid negative consequences.

Did you come to school to see some of your friends? Or because you like some of your subjects? If so, your choices were made because you thought that there would be positive consequences.

Often our choices are made both to escape negative consequences and to get positive consequences. What decision have you made that tried to avoid some things and gain others?

Maybe you went to a good movie so that you could get out of a bad day at home.

Perhaps you helped two of your friends make up after a fight so that you could enjoy them and not have to put up with their fighting.

Now—let's review for a moment. The points that have been made so far are: (1) you are responsible for your own acts; (2) you make choices because of negative and positive consequences. Many people have trouble accepting the first idea—that they are responsible for their own acts. Think about this question. Could anyone make you do something that you absolutely did not want to do? An easy answer to that is yes, if they physically forced me to do something. Okay, that is one weakness in the argument. But in most things we do, we are not physically forced. But, you say, sometimes there are negative consequences. You are right. You can choose to accept the negative consequences.

Many people do not accept responsibility for their own decisions. We call these people *losers*. Listen to the kinds of things they say:

- "I cheated on the test because the teacher was unfair."
- "I'm just like my mother. She weighs too much, and so do I."
- "The teacher just didn't teach the subject well enough for me to understand it."
- "People pick on me because I'm rich."
- "I didn't have a chance because I'm poor."
- "It wasn't my fault. I just went along with the gang."

Blamers! That's what losers are. They blame others for their own faults. No wonder—it is easier to blame others than to admit responsibility for our faults.

There are people who do take responsibility for their own faults and behaviors. We call them *winners*. Listen to the winners talk:

- "I cheated because I was too lazy to study. Next time I'll study harder."
- "I weigh too much because I eat too much. I'm going on a diet!"
- "If I had studied harder, I could have learned the subject."
- "People pick on me because I am really an unkind person. It's time for me to learn to be nicer."
- "I'm poor, but I could overcome it. I'll develop a plan."
- "How stupid can I be! The next time I'm with that bunch I'm not going to be led by the nose."

The bottom line on all this is simple. As long as you blame others for your problems, you are going to be a loser. You can choose to become a winner instead. To become a winner, here are the first two steps you need to take:

1. Learn to believe that you are responsible for your own acts.

2. Learn to make decisions that will result in gaining positive consequences and avoiding negative consequences.

You may be asking, "Why should I become a winner? I like being a loser." To answer your question, let's look at the likely consequences of behaving like a loser:

Positive Consequences of Being a Loser

■ You may fool yourself into believing you're happy

■ You don't have to take any risks

Negative Consequences of Being a Loser

■ You may feel insecure

■ You likely are unhappy inside

■ You may lose a lot of friends—except for the few people who also like to blame a lot

■ Being a blamer all the time is boring

■ Your parents will likely treat you like a child and give you little freedom

Now let's look at the likely consequences of behaving like a winner:

Positive Consequences of Being a Winner

■ Feel good about yourself

■ Know how to change your faults into positive actions

■ Are more likely to succeed in many areas of life

■ Have more true friends— people like other people who are cheerful

■ Your parents are likely to treat you like an adult and give you more responsibilities and more freedom

Negative Consequences of Being a Winner

■ Sometimes it hurts to look at your faults

■ Sometimes winners get "swelled heads"—and then you could lose friends

Consider each list. Would you change these lists? How? Would you rather behave like a winner or a loser?

Are you a blamer? Are you a loser? Some people associate being a winner with making a lot of money, having nice cars and houses, or being famous. There are a lot of losers who have and are all those things. The true winners admit their faults. They accept responsibility for their own acts. We believe that some people drink or take drugs so they can blame their failures on coke, booze, or some other substance. How nice it is not to take any responsibility.

Losers say, "The school failed me, I didn't flunk out." Or "He was a real bad teacher. Who could learn anything in that class?" We are not saying that there are not bad schools and teachers. We are saying that once you reach the point in your life when you can take care of yourself, you should stop blaming others. You should accept responsibility for your life.

Okay! Let's get back to the question, "Are you in charge of your life?" We believe that if you are old enough to be thinking about leaving school, you are ready to admit, "I am in charge of my life." Now comes the hard part. If I am in charge *and* I am a winner, then I have to admit that it's my decision to drop out. And I cannot blame anyone else for it. Also, *I* will be responsible for the consequences.

Do I Have Automatic Thoughts That Are Wrong?

Did you know that you develop thinking habits much the same way that you develop eating or sleeping habits? Just as you always order a hamburger with catsup and pickle, you automatically respond to certain ideas. Try the following exercise: On the left is a number of words or phrases. On the right is a row of blank spaces. Read the words on the left. On the right, fill in the first thought that comes to your mind in the blank spot.

1. It's Miller time   1. _____

2. Golden arches   2. _____

3. We do chicken right   3. _____

4. The Pepsi generation   4. _____

The words on the left were taken from commercials. Advertising people want you to think of certain pictures when you hear these words. They pay million of dollars to develop these automatic thoughts. Of course, other advertisers pay millions to have you think other thoughts.

For the most part, you learn your automatic thoughts without television or radio. Look at the following words on the left. Then write your first thought in the right-hand column:

1. School

2. Teachers

3. Homework

4. Books

5. Tests

1. _____

2. _____

3. _____

4. _____

5. _____

The words above are the ones you link to school. Look at the words you have written. Are they mostly positive or mostly negative? It's likely that if you are thinking of leaving school, they are mostly negative. Most people leave school to avoid negative consequences and to move toward positive consequences. Or so they think.

Remember in the beginning we said that people make mistakes in their thinking. Well, they do so because they do not question their automatic thoughts. (Is school really all bad?) They do not get enough information about the future. (Are just good things going to happen when you leave school?)

Let's redo the exercises on school with a different set of directions. This time, don't just write your first idea about the word. Think about what is good *and* bad about it.

1. School

Good _____

Bad _____

2. Teachers

Good _____

Bad _____

3. Homework

Good _____

Bad _____

4. Books   Good _____

                   Bad _____

5. Tests   Good _____

                   Bad _____

You may have had some trouble thinking of good things about school or tests. That's okay. *The idea is not to think automatically.* Now let's do the same thing. That is, list your good and bad thoughts associated with some other ideas.

1. Dropping out of   Good _____
   school

                     Bad _____

2. Going to work   Good _____

                     Bad _____

That's enough of this for now. We want to have you move ahead because some of you get bored. Some may not see that this has anything to do with your life right now. To sum up, don't let your automatic thoughts about school take you down the wrong track.

Where Did I Get My Basic Beliefs About School?

How did you develop your basic beliefs about school? No one can really answer that question for you. We know, though, that a lot of our ideas about the world come from our parents and relatives. In the spaces listed below, fill in the first names of your parents, grandparents, aunts, uncles, and cousins. Then put a "D" after their name if they dropped out of school and a "G" if they graduated. Put a D or G in [ ].

Parents _____ [ ] _____ [ ]

Stepparents _____ [ ] _____ [ ]

Grandparents _____ [ ] _____ [ ] _____ [ ] _____ [ ]

Aunts/ _____ [ ] _____ [ ] _____ [ ] _____ [ ]

Uncles _____ [ ] _____ [ ] _____ [ ] _____ [ ]

Cousins _____ [ ] _____ [ ] _____ [ ] _____ [ ]

_____ [ ] _____ [ ] _____ [ ] _____ [ ]

How many of the people in your family tree dropped out of school? Can you remember what they told you about school? Could they have planted some automatic thoughts?

Next list the same people below, beginning with your parents. Now fill in the jobs that they now hold. Put each person's job in [   ].

Parents _____ [   ] _____ [   ]

Stepparents _____ [   ] _____ [   ]

Grandparents _____ [   ] _____ [   ] _____ [   ] _____ [   ]

Aunts/ _____ [   ] _____ [   ] _____ [   ] _____ [   ]

Uncles _____ [   ] _____ [   ] _____ [   ] _____ [   ]

Cousins _____ [   ] _____ [   ] _____ [   ] _____ [   ]

_____ [   ] _____ [   ] _____ [   ] _____ [   ]

Can you see a pattern? Are the dropouts doing better? Worse?

Relatives, including grandparents and parents, are important in shaping our beliefs about school. They also help us develop basic beliefs about the rest of the world. Let's look at your basic beliefs about life.

What Are Your Basic Beliefs?

Basic beliefs are those things that you believe above all else. We all have basic beliefs about our country. These are taught to us in school, at home, through radio and television, in church, and in a number of other places. We also have basic beliefs about the importance of our family, money, power, being recognized by others, and having a good time.

Before you make any kind of choice it's important to think about your basic beliefs. Sometimes we get so unhappy about a situation, we forget what we believe. At other times, we just don't listen to ourselves.

Let's begin this part by having you find your basic beliefs about a number of areas.

Basic Belief—What Is Important to Me Is:

	Yes	No	Uncertain
1. Having a lot of money	_____	_____	_____
2. Being recognized as successful	_____	_____	_____
3. Having power over others	_____	_____	_____
4. Making a comfortable living	_____	_____	_____
5. Having control over my time	_____	_____	_____
6. Having a happy family	_____	_____	_____
7. Being able to get ahead	_____	_____	_____
8. Being secure—having a good job with a good income	_____	_____	_____

	Yes	No	Uncertain
9. Having time to do fun activities such as fishing or watching television	___	___	___
10. Change—not doing the same thing all the time	___	___	___
11. Being able to work on something new or original	___	___	___
12. Having a nice car	___	___	___
13. Living in a good house	___	___	___
14. Playing a musical instrument	___	___	___
15. Dancing or other artistic activity	___	___	___
16. Having a lot of friends	___	___	___
17. Getting along with my relatives	___	___	___
18. Having possessions—clothes, jewelry	___	___	___
19. Being able to write well	___	___	___
20. Being able to speak well	___	___	___
21. Being thought of as a smart person	___	___	___
22. Being physically attractive	___	___	___
23. Being healthy and in good shape	___	___	___
24. Participating in religious activities	___	___	___
25. Helping others	___	___	___
26. Having clean air and water—the environment	___	___	___

Now think about what you have done. In the following list, rank that thing that is most important to you by placing a 1 by the area that represents your most important basic belief, a 2 by your second most important belief, and so on.

_____ Money

_____ Family

_____ Religion

_____ Power over others

_____ Control over my own life

_____ Personal recognition and achievement

_____ Leisure (Fun)

_____ Physical attractiveness

_____ Helping others

Above, you listed your basic beliefs in order of their importance to you. Let's test this another way. You just received $5,000 and you must use this money to make sure that your life will be filled with the things you value most. You could use the entire $5,000 to make sure that you will always have money in your life. You could also use it to make sure that you have a family. Or you could split it up and put $3,000 on family and $2,000 on money. Do *not* think that because you have money, everything else will fall into place. A lot of people have that automatic thought, but we all know very rich people who are very unhappy. *Now* spend your $5,000 to make sure that the things you value most will be a part of your life.

List Beliefs   **Amount of Money Invested**

_____   _____

_____   _____

_____   _____

_____   _____

_____   _____

_____   _____

Total: $5,000

Did you get the same list as you did before? Why? Why not?

Why all this work about your basic beliefs or values? Because people who do not follow their basic beliefs end up being unhappy. If you believe that it is important to be married and have children, you will probably be unhappy if you don't eventually have a family. On the other hand, if money is important to you and you are unable to get it, you are likely to be very unhappy. Or if you cannot get money honestly, you may turn to dishonest means to get it. Some teenagers make $2000 a week selling cocaine. Of course, their chances of living a long time or staying out of jail are not good. Is money more important than a long life? It is for some people.

Basic beliefs are important because you need to consider them whenever you make important choices—like dropping out or staying in school. You may not like education. Yet you may need education to gain those things in life that you want. Earlier, it was said that people should view education as poverty insurance. Well, others should view it as mental health insurance. If you cannot get the things that you want, you are likely to be a very unhappy person. This doesn't mean that you are going to go crazy or need long-term counseling. But it can mean feeling bad about yourself, those around you, and the world in general. Who needs to go through life with that kind of attitude?

Basic Beliefs and What Turns Us On

Remember that we talked about behavior as either moving toward or away from positive or negative consequences. Well, some negative consequences are negative for everyone. A loud noise, someone on your back yelling at you, or someone saying you're no good are negatives for everyone. However, much of what each of us calls negative or positive comes from our basic beliefs—the things that we think either are or are not important. What follows are two lists of things to do. Compare each pair and circle the one you would choose:

1. Listening to rock 'n roll   vs.   Listening to a symphony orchestra
2. Visiting an art exhibit   vs.   Going to an auto show
3. Watching television   vs.   Listening to the radio
4. Being with friends   vs.   Being alone
5. Working indoors   vs.   Working outdoors
6. Going to a basketball game   vs.   Going to a soccer game
7. Spending time hanging out   vs.   Playing in a game
8. Saving money   vs.   Spending money
9. Having children   vs.   Not having children
10. Being good looking   vs.   Being smart
11. Studying   vs.   Working at a job
12. Eating Chinese food   vs.   Eating Mexican food
13. Taking chances   vs.   Playing it safe
14. Being in charge ("the boss")   vs.   Working in a group where everyone makes a decision
15. Being secure (no worries)   vs.   Living on the edge—taking risks

What you circled in each pair shows some of your basic beliefs. In real life, if given the chance, you will move toward things related to these beliefs. It will be those choices that you will see as offering positive consequences. Also, you will move away from things that are not related to your basic beliefs because you see them as negative.

At this time, you may be thinking, "school is negative (bad). So education must not be one of my basic beliefs." Perhaps that's true. But sometimes we have to put up with some things we do not like to get the things that we want. Why? No one is really sure why the world works that way. It just does.

Here is what's hard if you do not like school. Education can help protect you from some of the following things that most people do not like, such as:

■ Not being able to get a job

■ Being poor

■ Having a dull job

■ Having to work very, very hard to make a living

■ Having an attitude—being unhappy about your job

■ Being the last hired and the first fired

On the other hand, education can allow you to move toward these things:

■ More things for yourself, such as clothes, cars, houses

■ More happiness, because you can give things to those you love

■ Satisfaction, because you are doing things you enjoy

■ More self-respect

Again, we are not saying that just because you are dropping out of school, things are going to be terrible. It is interesting that many people who drop out of school eventually get a high school diploma. Why? Because they discovered they made a big mistake. It is also true that many people drop out of high school and do very well.

But, you need to know your basic beliefs. You need to know if it is going to take a high school education to get the things you want out of life. If dropping out will keep you from moving toward those things you want, then it is a mistake.

PUTTING IT ALL TOGETHER

It is time to be honest by answering the following questions:

1. Can I control my own life?

2. Am I in charge of my own life now?

3. Do I have automatic thoughts about school that are wrong?

4. What are my basic beliefs about life? Work? Leisure (Fun)?

5. Do I need an education to satisfy any of these basic beliefs?

If you are in charge of your own life, what are you doing with that power? Maybe you have decided that you don't really matter very much. That means you have handed the power to control yourself to others. Perhaps they make your decisions, including the one to stay or leave school. How sure are you that they know what is good for you?

Maybe you have decided not to do anything with the power you have over yourself. You have decided to just ride along and see what happens. That may work. Something very good may drop out of the sky. It has for a lot of people. And then, something good may *not* happen.

Maybe you have taken the power that you have over your own life and decided to hurt yourself no matter what. Sound strange? It isn't! People hurt themselves all the time with drugs, alcohol, driving too fast, and suicide. But sometimes they decide to hurt themselves in other ways. They decide to do what people expect. "My mother says I'm a bum. I'll be a bum." "My teacher calls me a criminal. I'll show him what a criminal I can be."

What are you doing with the power over your life? Are your automatic thoughts about school and self getting in the way? Do you stop to think, "Do I really believe what I think about myself, school, jobs, country? Or are these just ideas that I picked up along the way that need to be thrown away?"

If you think school is bad, you are wrong. It may be dull. Or hard work. But school is not bad. If you think something is wrong with you because you don't do well in school or you don't like school, you are also wrong. Some very famous people not only didn't like school, they didn't do very well in school.

Do you know what your basic beliefs are? Is an education an important step in getting the things you want out of life?

Maybe you are not sure what you want out of life. The chapters that follow will help you make some of those basic choices. Where do you want to be in one year? Three? Five? Ten? What would you like to have others say about the way you lived your life? About the things you did?

Up to this point, we have just been trying to stir up your interest and get you to thinking about yourself. Now, the serious business begins.

CHAPTER

3

MAKING DECISIONS

In some ways, the first part of this chapter is like chapter 2, because we are going to begin by looking at how you make decisions. How you make choices says a lot about you as a person. It says whether you believe you are in charge of your life, no matter what your beliefs are and no matter what you think of yourself.

Let's begin by looking at *how* people make decisions. The following describes four basic approaches:

1. *Thoughtful.* You know some of these people. You may be one yourself. Thoughtful decision makers define the problem that they are trying to deal with and then carefully collect facts about the different ways to solve it. If they are buying a used car, they read auto magazines to see which cars are best, drive several cars, have them checked out by a mechanic, crawl under the cars, and inspect their engines. They compare different cars and look at what they are getting for their money.

2. *Intuitive.* You also know some of these people. When they are faced with a problem, they seem to know what to do even if it is wrong. They may do many of the things that the thoughtful decision maker does. However, these people trust their "gut"—what they believe or sense about the right decision. Sometimes

they ignore facts. If they are buying a used car, they may buy the car based on how they feel about the car rather than the information they have collected.

3. *Dependent.* Maybe you know dependent decision makers, maybe not. These people cannot make up their minds. They ask everyone what to do. Worse, they cave into pressure to make a certain decision. These people rely on others to make their decisions. Why? It is usually because they do not trust themselves. If they are going to buy a used car, they will find out what their parents or friends think. They'll do what their parents or friends say, even if it doesn't agree with what they believe.

4. *Impulsive.* These people hate to make decisions. They get *very* nervous when they have to make one. They make decisions as quickly as possible just to get the decision made. They will buy the first car that comes along just to get the choice over with, so they may buy a loser.

The thoughtful approach to making choices is the best. The intuitive approach is also a fairly good way. Dependent or impulsive decision makers often make bad choices. Dependent decision makers may make good choices, though, as long as they depend on the right people. However, they often feel bad about what they decide. They know that they have given up control of their own lives. If they get help from bad decision makers, they make bad choices.

There are times when it really doesn't matter which way you use to make a decision. Let's say that you are choosing which candy bar to buy. If you buy a Snickers instead of a Mounds bar, 15 minutes later you have enjoyed your candy and you feel pretty much the same. In making such a choice, you may be thoughtful, intuitive, dependent, or impulsive.

There are other kinds of choices that demand thoughtful decisions. Look at the following choices. List the negative consequences of making a bad decision.

Decision   **Negative Consequences**

Punching a 275-pound football player   _____

Cheating on your boyfriend/girlfriend   _____

Taking a drug such as cocaine or LSD   _____

Stealing a watch   _____

"Sleeping around"   _____

You've probably figured out that thoughtful decisions need to be made whenever *bad* things can happen to you as a result of making bad decisions.

WHY DO PEOPLE MAKE BAD DECISIONS?

There are lots of reasons why people do not make good choices. First, making good decisions is hard work. Yes, good decision making takes work to think about the choices and to get the facts straight. It is easier just to drift or fall into a choice.

Second, some people don't make good decisions because they don't have confidence in themselves. These people feel worthless. They feel that they have no rights. They see others as prettier, healthier, smarter, more handsome, and just plain better. You have rights! The main right that you have is to make your own decisions. If you are going to make a mistake, it ought to be your mistake. But you won't be able to blame others.

Third, people make bad decisions because they do not know how to make good ones. You are not going to be one of these people. You are now going to learn how to make good decisions.

A THOUGHTFUL APPROACH
TO DECISION MAKING

Before you make a decision, you must see that there is a problem that needs to be solved—a choice to be made. The first step is to define the situation. The following are some problems that many young people (and some older people) have:

1. I don't have many friends.
2. I don't make enough money.
3. I don't date, but I would like to.
4. I am failing three subjects.

Once you know what the problem is, the second step is to write out how you would like things to be. What you are doing is setting goals that fit in with your basic beliefs. Some students have set the following goals:

1. I want to have at least two friends.
2. I want to earn $30 per week.
3. I would like to have one date per week.
4. I want to pass all my subjects.

SETTING GOALS

What has happened is clear. Each of these students first described his or her situation as it is. Then each set a goal for how he or she would like it to be. Let's talk more about setting goals.

A number of skills are needed to set goals for our lives. In this part of the book we will talk about these skills and work on them.

You may be asking, "How do I decide what my goals should be?" You begin by looking at those areas of your life that need change. To become a winner, you need to believe that you can make changes in your life. As we said earlier, if you choose instead to be a loser, you're likely to sit around blaming others. That's because the changes you would like to see haven't happened. Winners know that changes don't just happen—winners *make* changes happen. List some things about your life that you would like to *change:*

Things I Want to Work on Changing Now:

1. _____

2. _____

3. _____

4. _____

Now let's talk about the parts of a goal. The first part of a goal clearly states what RESULTS you would like to see. The second part states how much TIME you will allow yourself to see those results. The third part states your PLANS for reaching the goal. The last part states how you will measure your PROGRESS in order to decide that you have reached your goal.

Let's look at an example of goal setting for one possible change: improving poor study habits. We need the four parts: results, time, plans, progress. First, what results do we want? Here are some ideas:

1. I will learn at least one new way of studying.

2. I will know what is good about the way I study now and what study habits need improving.

Second, what about time? Goals can be thought of as short-term and long-term goals. It is important to make short-term goals that require you to make only a small amount of progress in a short amount of time. If you can reach a number of short-term goals, your confidence can grow. You can think more like a winner. For now, let's work on only one-week goals.

Third, let's look at how you can reach the goals you set. What should be the parts of your plan? Clearly you will need some facts about study skills. There are several ways to get these facts. You could attend a class on study habits. You could read a book about study skills. You could talk to your teacher about how to improve your study habits. You could also ask some of your classmates who do well in school to help you learn how to study better. Any of the above ways could be part of your plan.

Last, you need to decide if you have made enough progress toward your goal. Here are some ways you can measure your progress:

1. I will be able to describe one way of studying to my teacher in a satisfactory way.

2. I will have completed all the pages in a study skills book.

3. I will have received a passing grade in history this grading period.

All of these are different ways you can check your progress. Now let's put all the parts of the goal together:

Change: Poor Study Habits

In one week, I will know what is good about the way I study now and what study habits I need to improve. To reach this goal, I will watch a videotape on improving my study habits. I will measure my progress by being sure that I try two of the ideas that are presented. Also, I will ask my counselor or a teacher to review my work with me to see if she or he can offer any other help.

Now try writing goals for one of the things that you wish to change. Go back to the changes you said you wanted to work on. Remember, your goals must have all four parts— *results, time, plans, progress.*

Thing I Want to Change: _____

Goal—*Results I want to reach:*

_____

_____

_____

_____

How much time will I need:

One week _____

What are the possible plans for reaching the goal?

_____

_____

_____

How will I measure my progress?

_____

_____

Which of my basic beliefs is involved?

_____

_____

Is this goal in line with my basic beliefs?

_____

_____

REACHING YOUR GOAL

You have set your goal. Now we need to talk about following through on the plans you have made. First you need to discover the forces that will help you reach your goal. These can be internal (inside you) or external (outside you). External forces may be people, videotapes, books, work, and so on. Internal forces are your hopes to gain something positive or escape something negative. Remember, we are always moving toward positive consequences or away from negative ones.

Suppose one of your plans is to study one hour each night. What forces might *help* you to study at least one hour every night? What forces might *stop* you from studying one hour every night? Here's a possible list:

Forces that Can Help Me:

- I could ask Mom/Dad to remind me. (People)
- If I study more, I might get better grades. (Positive consequence)
- If I don't study more, I might flunk out and I want to graduate. (Avoid negative consequence and gain positive consequence)
- If I stick to my goal, I'll reward myself by going to a movie this weekend. (Positive consequence)
- I could view a film on studying.

Forces that May Block Me:

- Studying is too dull.
- I'm so dumb it really doesn't matter how much I study. (Loser talk)
- My friends may call up and ask me to go out with them, and I'd be afraid to say no because they wouldn't want to be my friends anymore. (Loser talk)
- My friends don't study; why should I? (Loser talk)
- I'm too lazy to study.

Now list the forces that could help you make a change or block you from changing the goal that you established on the previous worksheet:

Goal: _____

Forces that Can Help Me:

1. _____

2. _____

3. _____

4. _____

Forces that May Block Me:

1. _____

2. _____

3. _____

4. _____

Look at the list of forces that could block you. What could you do about them? Are any of them just excuses—things that losers would say? Are there things that other people can help you do? Your counselor? Your teachers? Your friends? One of your parents? One thing is for sure: If you're planning to make changes in one of your poor habits, you are going to need a lot of help. Below, list the people who could help you reach your first goal by offering you praise, teaching you new skills, or rewarding you in some way. State how they could help.

People Who Could Help Me Reach My Goals:

1. _____

2. _____

3. _____

4. _____

How They Can Help:

_____

_____

_____

_____

Now list on the next page the people who might block you from reaching your goals. State how they might block you.

People Who Could Block Me From Reaching My Goals: **How They Can Hurt:**

1. _____   _____

2. _____   _____

3. _____   _____

4. _____   _____

Different people can help you in different ways. Some of your friends may be great to party with, but they may not be able to help you reach your goals. Other friends may be helpful in reaching your goals. Your parents or other adults may help you gain positive consequences (the car, extra allowance, praise), or they may threaten you with negative consequences which you'd like to escape (some kind of punishment no dates, no phone calls).

Now think about the positive consequences that would result if you reached your goal. List them below:

Positive Consequences if I Reach My Goal:

1. _____

2. _____

3. _____

4. _____

Now list the negative consequences if you don't reach your goal:

Negative Consequences if I Don't Reach My Goal:

1. _____

2. _____

3. _____

4. _____

What about reading or watching something that might help you reach your goal? For instance, this book may help you learn how to set goals. Other books and videotapes are made on a number of subjects, such as how to study better, how to pick a career, or how to communicate better with your parents. List below any books or videotapes you could read or watch to help you reach your goal (ask your teacher, counselor, or librarian to help you if you are stuck):

Booklets I Can Read: **Videotapes I Can Watch:**

_____   _____

_____   _____

_____   _____

Finally, think about the ways you could reward yourself if you do reach your goal. And then think about the ways you could punish yourself if you don't reach your goal. You may be saying, ''You're crazy if you think I'm going to punish myself! I am not going to ground myself, or study an extra hour!'' Well, hopefully you won't have to. You'd only punish yourself if you did not reach your goal. Plus, you can think of the punishments as negative consequences that you can escape by reaching your goal.

Rewards I Can Give Myself if I Reach My Goal:

1. _____

2. _____

3. _____

4. _____

Punishments if I Don't Reach My Goal:

1. _____

2. _____

3. _____

4. _____

REVIEW

It is review time. We talked about becoming a winner by learning how to set goals. We talked about the four parts of a goal. List the four parts below:

1. _____

2. _____

3. _____

4. _____

Next, we talked about the forces that can help you to follow through with your plans to reach your goals. List the kinds of forces that can help you:

1. _____

2. _____

3. _____

So far, we have looked only at short-term goal setting. In the next chapter, we will look at long-term goal setting. We will also give you practice in setting both long- and short-term goals. The next chapter will deal with some long-term goal setting.

4

SETTING LIFE GOALS

In this chapter, we want you to begin to think about your life like a winner. We want you to think about taking charge of your future and making positive things happen.

THIS IS YOUR DREAM LIFE

For your first step, you need to dream about your future—to build a dream of your fantasy life. This may make you uncomfortable, because you may believe that students don't dream. Sure they do! Remember the last time you daydreamed in class?

Or maybe you're saying, "Why dream about a world that I know can't come true?" How do you know? Lots of songs were once dreams in a songwriter's mind! New dress designs, car designs, poems—in fact all new creations begin as someone's fantasy or dream. How do they get from fantasy to reality? Time, energy, work—and sometimes a little luck. Thinking like a winner can help you to spend the time and energy you need to make your dreams come true. So think like a winner, and start building your dream life. Ready?

Let's divide your life up into five parts. Write your list on the following worksheet. First, think about your ideal educational future. What new things would you like to learn? There are all kinds of schools to choose from. Of course you may decide that the ideal dream is no more school. Whatever you choose—it's really your ideal future.

Second, think about an ideal future career, the one you would like. Would you like to discover oil wells? Would you like to be so rich you'll go around giving money away? Remember that most people, whether they're rich or poor, choose to work. Where would you most like to work? What would you most like to do at work? How much money would you like to earn? How much time off? Would you choose an unusual career—like a male nurse or a female truck driver? Whatever you decide, it's your ideal.

Next, what's your ideal of the close relationships you will have with others in the future? Would you like to remain single for a few years? Several years? Many years? Perhaps you never want to get married! If you do marry, would you like to marry early? Do you want to have children? How many? Would you like to live together with friends in a big house? Would you like to live with just one close friend? Think about what you'd most like to do.

Fourth, think about the ideal way to spend your leisure time. How would you like to play as an adult? Bowl three times a week? Travel all over the world? Tan on the beach and play in the surf? Volunteer to work in a hospital, or coach a kids' baseball team? Your time away from your work is yours to plan in the most ideal way possible.

Last, how about your ideal of your life in your church group or community? Would you like to be a leader in your church or community? Perhaps these things will not be an important part of your life. It's up to you!

Got your dream life planned? Think it over now. Anything you want to change? There's room on the following worksheet for you to write out your dreams.

My Ideal Future

EDUCATION:

_____

_____

_____

_____

CAREER:

_____

_____

_____

_____

CLOSE RELATIONSHIPS:

_____

_____

_____

_____

LEISURE (FUN):

_____

_____

_____

_____

RELIGION AND COMMUNITY:

_____

_____

_____

_____

THIS IS YOUR REAL LIFE

OK, you've planned your ideal future. Now we want you to dream again. But this time, consider what you really think will happen in your life as you now see it.

Let's first look at your educational future. Will you graduate from high school? Get a college diploma? Go to a technical school?

Second, look ahead into your life and think about your career. What job will you hold? How much money do you really think you will make? What do you think you will be doing at your job? Will you enjoy it?

Third, think about your future close relationships. Will you stay single or marry? Get divorced? How many children will you have? Where will you live?

Fourth, what will your leisure life be like? How much time and money will you really have to spend?

Fifth, what does your future in church groups and in your community look like? How active will you be?

Record all your answers on the following worksheet. If you get stuck in some of these areas, ask your teacher, counselor, or librarian for help. They have books, such as the *Occupational Outlook Handbook,* which describes different jobs, the amount of education you need to get each job, and the money you would earn for each job.

My Real Future

EDUCATION:

_____

_____

_____

CAREER:

_____

_____

_____

CLOSE RELATIONSHIPS:

_____

_____

_____

LEISURE (FUN):

_____

_____

_____

RELIGION AND COMMUNITY:

_____

_____

_____

Now, you have just completed two dream exercises. You also should have two lists completed: (1) My Ideal Future and (2) My Real Future. Perhaps your lists look something like this:

	My Ideal Future	**My Realistic Future**
Education:	complete high school go to college medical school	complete high school secretarial training
Career:	medical doctor $150,000	executive secretary $15,000
Family:	marry late-rich wealthy 2 children	marry earlier, girl/boy down the street 2 children
Leisure:	The country club golf travel-Europe	local basketball games beach in the summer
Community/ Religious Activities:	a leader influential	a follower in the community a leader in my church

Now look at your two lists. Are they different? List as many reasons as you can for the differences between your ideal future and your real future. Your list might appear as follows:

1. Was not born rich

2. Was not born smart

3. Too lazy in school

4. Poor Study habits

5. Behind in school

6. Poor decision making ability

7. Not handsome/pretty enough

Be very thorough!

My List

1. _____

2. _____

3. _____

4. _____

5. _____

6. _____

7. _____

Remember our talk about winners and losers? Now go back through your list. How many of your reasons are really excuses? How many times are you trying to pass the blame on other people or circumstances? Are you thinking like a loser? Look at the list we made. Being born poor will not keep you from going to medical school, though it will make it harder. Having average intelligence may keep you from going to medical school, but some with average intelligence have made it.

To repeat, make a note of those reasons that you are simply blaming others. Ask yourself this question: "Am I accepting responsibility for my own life?"

The Immediate Future: High School Graduation

One part of your future that is more immediate than others is your schooling. You are in school now, even though you may be quitting soon. *Question:* If you quit school, who must accept responsibility for that action? *Answer:* You must!

Remember we talked about consequences. What would be the consequences of staying in school? What would be the consequences of dropping out of school? Also think about your ideal and real future. Was one of the differences between the two how much schooling you would need to reach one or the other?

Schooling is important! You have heard that over and over again. However, school is only important if you decide that it is important to you. That means school is important to other people. Those other people may make a difference in your life. But you can accept responsibility for your own life. Make a decision and accept the negative and positive consequences of that decision.

Make a list of the positive consequences of finishing school:

1. _____

2. _____

3. _____

4. _____

5. _____

6. _____

7. _____

8. _____

9. _____

10. _____

Make a list of the negative consequences of finishing school:

1. _____

2. _____

3. _____

4. _____

5. _____

6. _____

7. _____

8. _____

9. _____

10. _____

Which list is longer? Are there more positive consequences than negative ones?

For now, we'd like you to decide that it is of value for you to graduate from high school. "I will graduate from high school" will be a goal for you (at least for the moment). Let's look now at the four parts of this goal.

We've already stated the RESULT—you want to graduate. Next, decide the TIME. How much time do you need to meet all the requirements? Third, what are they? These requirements can be your way of measuring your PROGRESS toward your goal. Measure your progress on the next page:

My Progress Toward Graduation

What I Need

_____ total credits

_____ credits in English

_____ credits in mathematics

_____ credits in science

_____ credits in social studies

_____ credits in physical education

_____ credits in vocational education

_____ days of attendance

_____ passing grade on competency test

My Progress So Far

_____ total credits

_____ credits in English

_____ credits in mathematics

_____ credits in science

_____ credits in social studies

_____ credits in physical education

_____ credits in vocational education

_____ days of attendance

_____ I passed competency test

_____ I did not pass competency test

Other Requirements

What I Need

_____

_____

_____

My Progress So Far

_____

_____

_____

Make sure your list is accurate and complete. Once it is finished, you should understand what you are going to have to do to get a high school diploma (reach your goal). Your goal may be to get a certificate of attendance, instead. Some schools give these to people who do not meet some of the requirements for graduation. What is it? Is it any good? Will it be as good as a high school diploma? Make sure you understand why some people get a diploma and others a certificate of attendance.

We have covered three parts of your goal for graduating; the last part is your PLAN for reaching that goal. To help you, we have made the following list of possible areas in which you may want to make some plans. Check where you need help.

Skills and/or Requirements Necessary for High School Graduation	Check if You Need Help
1. Basic skills (reading, math)	_____
2. Study skills	_____
3. Budgeting time	_____
4. Motivation	_____
5. Test-taking skills	_____
6. Passing the competency test	_____
7. Getting along with others	_____
8. Standing up to my friends who want me to quit	_____
9. Stopping drug and/or alcohol use	_____
10. Finding a job to support myself	_____
11. Gaining family support for school	_____
12. Premarital counseling—delaying marriage	_____

13. Family planning (dealing with
    pregnancy)   _____

14. Other_____   _____

Each area you checked can be part of the plan that will help you to reach your goal of graduating. For instance, if you checked study skills, you should write down what your plan is for getting help with your study skills. Do the same thing for other areas that you checked in the following space:

Skill   **Plan for Getting Help**

1. _____   _____

2. _____   _____

3. _____   _____

4. _____   _____

5. _____   _____

6. _____   _____

7. _____   _____

8. _____   _____

9. _____   _____

10. _____   _____

We talked before about forces that help people to reach their goals. Remember the four forces—people, self-help materials, rewards, and consequences (positive and negative). List on the next page at least four forces that will help you to graduate, and four forces that will block you.

Forces that Can Help Me Graduate:

1. _____

2. _____

3. _____

4. _____

Forces that May Block Me:

1. _____

2. _____

3. _____

4. _____

Read over your list of blocks. Do any of them sound like loser statements? You now know how to become a winner instead. So cross off the loser statements, and write them in winner talk instead. Change the blocks into forces that will help you take responsibility for your own behavior. Circle all the forces that will help you reach your goal.

We have looked at the forces that you can use to help you reach the goal of high school graduation. Next, we will give you a chance to "do your own thing." You can decide on your own goals in three areas of your life: education, career, and close relationships.

5

SETTING LONG-TERM LIFE GOALS

As we have already seen, many things influence our lives. Our parents, our teachers, our brains, and even some very unexpected things. In this chapter, we will begin to look at where you want to go and how to get there. Now, we will work on setting life goals in three areas: education, career, and close relationships. Later, we will learn how to reach those goals.

SETTING EDUCATIONAL GOALS

Let's start with education. Write out a list of education goals for yourself. For now, just write what RESULTS you want to reach in the time stated.

Educationally, where do you want to be in:

One month? _____

One year? _____

Five years? _____

Now take each of these goals and break it down in the following way. First, list all the forces that will help you reach that goal. Then list all the forces that might block you from reaching the goal.

One-month Goal

Forces that Can Help Me:

1. _____
2. _____
3. _____
4. _____
5. _____
6. _____
7. _____

Forces that May Block Me:

1. _____
2. _____
3. _____
4. _____
5. _____
6. _____
7. _____

One-year Goal

Forces that Can Help Me:

1. _____
2. _____
3. _____
4. _____
5. _____
6. _____
7. _____

Forces that May Block Me:

1. _____
2. _____
3. _____
4. _____
5. _____
6. _____
7. _____

Five-year Goal

Forces that Can Help Me:

1. _____
2. _____
3. _____
4. _____
5. _____
6. _____
7. _____

Forces that May Block Me:

1. _____
2. _____
3. _____
4. _____
5. _____
6. _____
7. _____

Go back through each of your goals and circle the forces that you can use in reaching your goal. Be sure to catch the "blaming" forces. Cross them out and write them again in winner talk. You should find you can use most of the forces. Remember, think like a winner!

Look over your goals again. Did you notice that your long- and short-term goals seemed to fit together in some way? Our lives are not divided up into separate parts. What we do now can help us or stop us from reaching our goals in the future. *Note:* If you do not reach your short-term goals, your long-term goals may not be reached either.

When you wrote your goals above, you only had two parts: results and time. Now write your plans for meeting both your short- and long-term educational goals. Also write how you will measure your progress. If you have no educational plans beyond dropping out or graduating from high school, stop there.

Plans for reaching my *one-month* educational goal:

Example: Improve all my grades.

_____

_____

How I will measure my progress:

Example: Check with teacher on my grades.

_____

_____

Plans for reaching my *one-year* educational goals:

Example: Pass all subjects in the 10th grade.

_____

_____

How I will measure my progress:

Example: Report card.

_____

_____

Plans for reaching my *five-year* educational goal:

Example: Complete a cosmetology course at a local community college.

_____

_____

How I will measure my progress:

Example: Pass the state examinations for cosmetologists.

_____

_____

Was making these plans hard? Planning the future is hard for many people. Some are not used to planning and need to learn more planning skills. For others, the future seems so big and scary that they are afraid to make plans. Your plans may not come true exactly as you wrote them. You may change your mind. You might come into wealth. A lot of things may happen: death, marriage, natural disaster, and ill health are a few. Think of some others.

The point here is that many things slow you down as you work toward your plans. Check and see if this is not true in your own life.

SETTING CAREER GOALS

Now, you should begin to set goals for your career. Let's repeat the same steps that we went through in setting your educational goals.

In terms of your career, write what RESULTS you want to reach in the time below:

One month?_____

One year?_____

Five years?_____

Setting career goals may be a lot harder for you than setting educational goals. The reason? There are many more things to think about. But you can divide these into several groups. These are:

1. *What kind of working conditions do I want?*

    a. Indoors or outdoors _____

    b. Work alone or with others _____

    c. Work with tools or ideas _____

    d. Work with facts or tools _____

    e. Work with ideas or people _____

    f. Suit and tie or work clothes _____

    g. Clean or dirty _____

    h. Noisy or quiet _____

2. *What are my skills?*

    a. Reading—high or low _____

    b. Math—high or low _____

    c. Using office machines—typewriters, calculators, computers—high or low _____

    d. Fixing things—engines, televisions—high or low _____

    e. Construction skills—carpentry, bricklaying—high or low _____

    f. Selling—high or low _____

    g. Meeting people—high or low _____

    h. Caring for people—high or low _____

    i. Operating equipment (e.g., tractors)—high or low _____

j. Cooking—high or low _____

k. Waiting on tables—high or low _____

l. Writing—high or low _____

m. Supervising others—high or low _____

n. Teaching people—high or low _____

o. Cleaning—high or low _____

p. Guarding/protecting—high or low _____

3. *How much money do I need to make now? How much will I need in five years? What will I need money for?*

	Now	5 years
Housing	_____	_____
Food/household supplies	_____	_____
Auto/transportation	_____	_____
Insurance	_____	_____
Utilities		
Telephone	_____	_____
Electricity	_____	_____
Gas	_____	_____
Water	_____	_____
Leisure (fun)	_____	_____
Miscellaneous	_____	_____

4. *What kinds of jobs are there for me?*

You will have to decide this on your own. But people who leave school, and even some high school graduates, often take the following kinds of jobs:

a.   Fast food restaurant worker (McDonald's, Burger King)

b.   Waiting on tables in a restaurant

c.   Short-order cook or kitchen helper

d.   Laborer in construction—help carpenters, electricians, clean up, dig trenches

e.   Retail sales—work in department store or grocery store accepting money for clothing or food (cashier)

f.   Custodian—work at cleaning up public and private businesses such as office buildings, hotels, schools (may be called maids in hotels)

g.   Attendants—work at service stations, car washes, toll booths, parking lots, accepting money and offering service

h.   Nurses aide and orderly in hospitals and nursing homes

i.   Truck driver—drive trucks long and short distances

j.   Food counter worker—serve food in department stores and cafeterias

k.   Guard—protect homes, factories, airports, offices

j.   Gardener and groundskeeper—plant shrubs, mow grass, trim shrubs

m.   Dining room and cafeteria worker—clean tables, serve food

Many of these jobs pay $4.00 to $6.00 per hour. Find out how much they pay in your area.

If you do not have a job at this time, visit businesses that are hiring. Try to find out if you can get a job. See if it offers the kinds of working conditions that you want and if it will allow you to earn enough money to meet basic expenses now. Find out if your earnings improve over time.

What are the forces that are working for and against reaching your goals?

One-month Goal

Forces that Can Help Me:

1. _____
2. _____
3. _____
4. _____
5. _____
6. _____
7. _____

Forces that May Block Me:

1. _____
2. _____
3. _____
4. _____
5. _____
6. _____
7. _____

One-year Goal

Forces that Can Help Me:

1. _____
2. _____
3. _____
4. _____
5. _____
6. _____
7. _____

Forces that May Block Me:

1. _____
2. _____
3. _____
4. _____
5. _____
6. _____
7. _____

Five-year Goal

Forces that Can Help Me:

1. _____
2. _____
3. _____
4. _____
5. _____
6. _____
7. _____

Forces that May Block Me:

1. _____
2. _____
3. _____
4. _____
5. _____
6. _____
7. _____

Now circle the forces that will help you reach your goals. Change any "blaming" blocks into winner talk, so you can use them to help you reach your goals.

Now write the PLANS and the PROGRESS parts of your goals:

Plans for *one-month* goal: _____

_____

How I will measure my progress: _____

_____

Plans for *one-year* goal: _____

_____

How I will measure my progress: _____

_____

Plans for *five-year* goal: _____

_____

How I will measure my progress: _____

_____

Now go back and look at the relationship between your education and career goals. *They should be related.* We know that both sets of plans must go hand in hand if career goals are to be reached. With this in mind, do you need to change either set of goals? Write out any changes that are needed.

_____

_____

_____

_____

_____

SETTING GOALS FOR CLOSE RELATIONSHIPS WITH PEOPLE

Now let's look at goals for close relationships. Close relationships are those with friends, parents, husbands, wives, and relatives. These goals may be different. However, a one-week goal might be to find out more about what makes a good relationship. Or it can be learning about the cost of raising a child so that you can consider family planning. Did you know that it may cost $100,000 to send a child to college in a few years?

Now what are your close-relationships goals in:

One month?_____

One year?_____

Five years?_____

Now list the forces for and against reaching these goals.

One-month Goal

Forces that Can Help Me:

1. _____
2. _____
3. _____
4. _____
5. _____
6. _____
7. _____

Forces that May Block Me:

1. _____
2. _____
3. _____
4. _____
5. _____
6. _____
7. _____

One-year Goal

Forces that Can Help Me:

1. _____
2. _____
3. _____
4. _____
5. _____
6. _____
7. _____

Forces that May Block Me:

1. _____
2. _____
3. _____
4. _____
5. _____
6. _____
7. _____

Five-year Goal

Forces that Can Help Me:

1. _____
2. _____
3. _____
4. _____
5. _____
6. _____
7. _____

Forces that May Block Me:

1. _____
2. _____
3. _____
4. _____
5. _____
6. _____
7. _____

Once again, circle the forces that you can use to help you reach your goals. Look at your "blocks," too, and see which ones are loser talk. Try to change these into winner talk so you can use them to help reach your goals, also.

Now write the PLANS and PROGRESS parts of your goals below:

Plans for *one-month* goal: _____

_____

_____

How I will measure my progress: _____

_____

_____

Plans for *one-year* goal: _____

_____

_____

How I will measure my progress: _____

_____

_____

Plans for *five-year* goal: _____

_____

_____

How I will measure my progress: _____

_____

_____

You may wish to finish the same steps for your leisure (fun life) and for the role you want to play in your community. Remember when you did your ideal and real life, you were asked to fill in these areas.

Leisure, or doing things just for fun, is very important in our lives. Many leisure activities cost money, but many do not. If you plan to buy a bass boat and fish, that costs money. So does attending a pro football or basketball game. Walking, watching television (if you have the set), and reading (if you check the books out of the library), cost very little money. If you want to try fun activities that cost money, you need to plan to make money on the job.

You now have a set of goals. You have also begun to build a plan for reaching these goals. Give yourself a pat on the back. You are ahead of most people your age—or of any age. And, you are also well on your way to becoming a winner!

We hope you will use this book again in the future to look at the goals you have set now and to help you decide how to reach certain future goals. It is likely your goals will change as you grow older. But as long as you have learned how to become a winner, you will be able to set new goals when you want to.

If your life plan means leaving school, you need to read chapter 6. It will teach you how to enter school again if you decide to do so later.

6

IF I LEAVE SCHOOL, WHAT'S MY EDUCATIONAL FUTURE?

Imagine that you leave school before graduation and you decide that you made a mistake. You want to go back to school! Hard to imagine. Yet 40 percent—4 in 10—of the people who drop out of school are just "stop outs," and they go back to finish high school or they enroll in a General Educational Development (GED) program. A GED program is designed to help dropouts develop basic educational skills (reading, math, and writing). Once these skills are learned and an exam is passed, a dropout can get a certificate (not a diploma). If you are going to drop out, you need to know what your alternatives are for getting more schooling.

ALTERNATIVE HIGH SCHOOLS

You may decide that you just cannot go to school each day for a lot of reasons. You may need to earn money to feed yourself or your family. You may not be able to get child care. Or you just may not want to put up with the usual high school day anymore.

Many cities and towns offer alternative high school programs for pupils who do not fit into the regular schools. Alternative schools may permit part-time study. They may offer evening courses. Often, alternative high schools allow students to work at their own pace rather than follow the lock-step ways that you are used to in regular classrooms.

Alternative high schools have been set up because administrators, teachers, and counselors want to help you finish high school. They know how important it is for you.

Often, people who drop out of high schools enroll in alternative schools right away. Others enroll after they have been out of high school for a while. You need to find out how you can enroll in the alternative school in your community, if one is available. Begin by completing the following information:

Name of Alternative School _____

Address _____

Telephone number _____

Contact person _____

Other information (schedule, types of programs offered, etc.) _____

_____

_____

_____

GED PROGRAMS

A GED program will inprove your basic educational skills. These programs are offered by colleges, vocational schools, and in some places, school districts. Your goal, should you sign up, is to pass the General Educational Development test. If you pass, you will be given a certificate that shows your skills are about the same as those of a high school graduate. On job applications, you may list that you have earned a GED instead of a high school diploma.

You should know that many employers do not think as much of the GED as they do a high school diploma. You should also know that you may not be as well prepared in reading, math, and writing if you pass a GED test as you would if you finished high school.

But some colleges accept the GED certificate for admission of students in place of the high school diploma. The GED can open many doors for you, both in the job market and in the educational arena.

STATE LEVEL EQUIVALENCY TESTS AND CERTIFICATES

Many states now offer students the opportunity to pass tests to show that they have gained the educational knowledge needed for graduation from high school. Your counselor can tell you if your state offers this choice.

Other states offer certificates for people who stay in school for certain lengths of time, even though they do not finish high school. Sometimes, these are called certificates of attendance.

You should know that certificates of attendance are not as highly regarded as high school diplomas, but they are far superior to dropping out with no certificate or diploma.

INDEPENDENT STUDY/ CORRESPONDENCE COURSES

Some universities, such as the University of Nebraska-Lincoln (UNL) and the University of Missouri, offer high school courses by mail. For example, at UNL you can enroll in ninth, tenth, eleventh, and twelfth grade English courses or take a basic electricity and electronics course by mail. The University of Missouri offers high school courses dealing with sociology, religion, psychology, personal development, history, government, geography, economics, mathematics, English, and other fields.

These courses can be used toward graduation from your local high school if they are accepted by a local school official, usually a counselor. If you decide to leave school and only need a few credits to graduate, you may wish to explore using these courses to finish your graduation requirements.

For information about the courses offered at UNL or the University of Missouri, you may write to the following addresses:

Center for Independent Study
136 Clark Hall
University of Missouri
Columbia, MO 65211

Independent Study High School
Division of Continuing Studies
Nebraska Center for Continuing Education
33rd and Holdrege St.
University of Nebraska-Lincoln
Lincoln, NE 68583-0900

Just remember that courses taken at these two centers or others must be preapproved by your counselor or principal. But independent study courses may allow you to earn your high school diploma.

OTHER PROGRAMS

Some public community colleges offer high school courses that may also allow you to finish high school if you drop out. There are also private schools that offer the same kinds of programs. These are likely to cost more. But if you can afford them and you think you would like them, go for it.

DROPPING BACK IN

Deciding to come back to school once you have dropped out can be hard for some. If you are black or Hispanic, you are less likely to go back to school once you leave. If you live in a large city or in a rural area, you are not as likely to go back. The same is true if you are female or poor. We are not exactly sure why these students are less likely to go back to school. It is possible that they liked school less than other students and so they stay out more often. It may also be true that females and minorities see less to be gained in education than white males.

No matter what the reason people stay out of school once they leave, every thought should be given to returning if you do leave and decide that you have made a mistake. Some of the alternative schools just mentioned have counseling services that will help you decide if school is for you once you leave. You should call the counselor or another school official to discuss returning to school.

Don't listen to your friends who dropped out. Sometimes these people just want you to be like them. It is your life. Throughout this book, it has been stated strongly that you need to take charge. Taking charge is what winning in life is all about. Sometimes when we take charge, we make mistakes. If you take charge of your life and drop out, that may turn out to be a mistake. If it is, correct it. Drop back in!

VGM CAREER BOOKS

OPPORTUNITIES IN
Available in both paperback and hardbound editions
Accounting Careers
Acting Careers
Advertising Careers
Aerospace Careers
Agriculture Careers
Airline Careers
Animal and Pet Care
Appraising Valuation Science
Architecture
Automotive Service
Banking
Beauty Culture
Biological Sciences
Biotechnology Careers
Book Publishing Careers
Broadcasting Careers
Building Construction Trades
Business Communication Careers
Business Management
Cable Television
Carpentry Careers
Chemical Engineering
Chemistry Careers
Child Care Careers
Chiropractic Health Care
Civil Engineering Careers
Commercial Art and Graphic Design
Computer Aided Design and Computer Aided Mfg.
Computer Maintenance Careers
Computer Science Careers
Counseling & Development
Crafts Careers
Culinary Careers
Dance
Data Processing Careers
Dental Care
Drafting Careers
Electrical Trades
Electronic and Electrical Engineering
Energy Careers
Engineering Careers
Engineering Technology Careers
Environmental Careers
Eye Care Careers
Fashion Careers
Fast Food Careers
Federal Government Careers
Film Careers
Financial Careers
Fire Protection Services
Fitness Careers
Food Services
Foreign Language Careers
Forestry Careers
Gerontology Careers
Government Service
Graphic Communications
Health and Medical Careers
High Tech Careers
Home Economics Careers
Hospital Administration
Hotel & Motel Management
Human Resources Management Careers
Industrial Design
Information Systems Careers
Insurance Careers
Interior Design

International Business
Journalism Careers
Landscape Architecture
Laser Technology
Law Careers
Law Enforcement and Criminal Justice
Library and Information Science
Machine Trades
Magazine Publishing Careers
Management
Marine & Maritime Careers
Marketing Careers
Materials Science
Mechanical Engineering
Medical Technology Careers
Microelectronics
Military Careers
Modeling Careers
Music Careers
Newspaper Publishing Careers
Nursing Careers
Nutrition Careers
Occupational Therapy Careers
Office Occupations
Opticiany
Optometry
Packaging Science
Paralegal Careers
Paramedical Careers
Part-time & Summer Jobs
Performing Arts Careers
Petroleum Careers
Pharmacy Careers
Photography
Physical Therapy Careers
Physician Careers
Plumbing & Pipe Fitting
Podiatric Medicine
Printing Careers
Property Management Careers
Psychiatry
Psychology
Public Health Careers
Public Relations Careers
Purchasing Careers
Real Estate
Recreation and Leisure
Refrigeration and Air Conditioning Trades
Religious Service
Restaurant Careers
Retailing
Robotics Careers
Sales Careers
Sales & Marketing
Secretarial Careers
Securities Industry
Social Science Careers
Social Work Careers
Speech-Language Pathology Careers
Sports & Athletics
Sports Medicine
State and Local Government
Teaching Careers
Technical Communications
Telecommunications
Television and Video Careers
Theatrical Design & Production
Transportation Careers

Travel Careers
Veterinary Medicine Careers
Vocational and Technical Careers
Welding Careers
Word Processing
Writing Careers
Your Own Service Business

CAREERS IN
Accounting
Advertising
Business
Communications
Computers
Education
Engineering
Health Care
Science

CAREER DIRECTORIES
Careers Encyclopedia
Occupational Outlook Handbook

CAREER PLANNING
Admissions Guide to Selective Business Schools
Career Planning and Development for College Students
  and Recent Graduates
Careers Checklists
Careers for Bookworms and Other Literary Types
Careers for Sports Nuts
Handbook of Business and Management Careers
Handbook of Scientific and Technical Careers
How to Change Your Career
How to Get and Get Ahead On Your First Job
How to Get People to Do Things Your Way
How to Have a Winning Job Interview
How to Land a Better Job
How to Make the Right Career Moves
How to Prepare for College
How to Run Your Own Home Business
How to Write a Winning Résumé
Joyce Lain Kennedy's Career Book
Life Plan
Planning Your Career of Tomorrow
Planning Your College Education
Planning Your Military Career
Planning Your Young Child's Education

SURVIVAL GUIDES
Dropping Out or Hanging In
High School Survival Guide
College Survival Guide

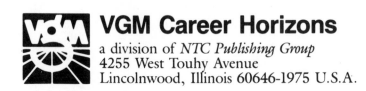 **VGM Career Horizons**
a division of *NTC Publishing Group*
4255 West Touhy Avenue
Lincolnwood, Illinois 60646-1975 U.S.A.